Air Breathes Light
Ellie Ann Deighton

Copyright © 2025 by Ellie Ann Deighton

All rights reserved.

No part of this publication may be reproduced, distributed, or transmitted in any form or by any means, including photocopying, recording, or other electronic or mechanical methods, without the prior written permission of the publisher, except as permitted by Australian copyright law. For permission requests or bulk orders, contact the author.

The story, all names, characters, and incidents portrayed in this production are fictitious. No identification with actual persons (living or deceased), places, buildings, and products is intended or should be inferred.

Book Cover by Ellie Ann Deighton

1st Edition 2025

Contents

Epigraph	1
Ellie's Light	2
Dedication	4
Foreword	7
1. Darkness.	13
2. Lightness.	29
3. Dark.	37
4. Light.	47
5. Shimmering.	67
6. Glimmering.	77
7. Shine.	85
8. Whole.	107
The Wheel Of Life	149
silver witch rose	159
About the author	160
Author's note	162

Intuitively Me 164

Acknowledgements 166

Apparently truth is a bitch
But truth is the wild one who sets us free
Truth is our reminder
We are all intuitive beings
We are connected across all of time and space
We keep forgetting
And then the truth hits us like a trickle of light or a soft breeze
Over and over
Until we listen and if we don't listen
We are hit
Tornado after tornado
Bright light that is too bright
We'd rather retreat into the darkness
Keep forgetting who we are
Keep losing ourselves in the muck of an unfulfilled life
Until we declare, 'Fuck it'
And we let the truth slap us
We shed the shame of shying away from ourselves
We grow wings
And suddenly we are free
~ evidence suggests

ELLIE'S LIGHT IN THE WORLD

FICTION
Ankhara Codes I: An Adventure to Essence
Ankhara Codes II: Allies of the Soul
Ankhara Codes III: A Devotion To Peace

ORACLE CARDS
Fruits of the Feminine

POETRY
'It' is GOLD
Fire Body Warm
Silver Witch Rose
Water River Run

NON-FICTION
Myths of a Mystic Woman

MUSIC ALBUMS
Temple Calling: An Album For Your Altar

ONLINE TRAININGS & COURSES:
Intuitively Me: The Wheel of Life {Air}
Sensual Essence: A Remembering Of Your Bliss {Fire}
The Remembering: Coven Membership {Silver}
Synchronise Me: Emotional Alchemy Training {Water}
Monetise Your Magic: Creative Mastermind {Gold}
Extrasensory: School of Light {Salt}
The Hatching Voice & Speaker Training {Earth}

more at elliedeighton.com

This is the fifth book of seven in The Elemental Collection; a poetry series focused on the seven essential elements of fulfilment.

You can read The Elemental Collection in any order you choose.

AIR BREATHES LIGHT

To you who shine brightly
And to you who have grown comfortably dim
When it comes to your light there is only one word:
More.

ELLIE ANN DEIGHTON

Foreword
In my journal I wrote...

June 22 2025

End result: To meet my muse and be informed of the calling of my heart; Air Breathes Light.

I am the magic
And the muse
And I am here
To say to you:

Air comes in
Through all the cracks
Even if you're hurting
And life's breaking your back
Air will still be there
As you can't keep out the light
This knowing in your being
Is like a fever in the night

First you'll just start sweating
You'll strip off what you're not
And then you'll have a breakthrough
You'll realise you're so hot
For things that bring you life and love
And not for obligation
You'll see the air is just your light
And helps you reach your greatness
So when you sweat and things get tough
And you're rolling in the darkness
It's not just 'bad', you're not just 'wrong'
You are dual and tasting life's harshness
Because that is real, the pain is there
You are wounded, you are human
But what else is real is all the air
Telling you what to do with
The wisdom in your heart and the knowing in your chest
The talents that you have to help you live your life the best
The air is always whispering
For the light is always within you
Your intuition is a natural thing
That the darkness tries to cage in you
But when you allow the dark to be there
And don't try to fight it with the light
You will naturally live a more glorious life
Letting go of the need to be right

Letting go of the need to figure it all out
Leaning into the need just to be
Letting go of the need to argue and shout
Leaning into the art of receiving
For the air equals the light
And the light equals the love
And we waste all this time seeing the separate
When you allow the air
And the light that you share
You can lean into the love you are meant for
And it's not just for you
It is equally of you
It's every little beat in your chest
Every cell of your body
Every inch of your being
In every divine street that you tread
The air guides you home
As it's your own damn light
And it carries the message of your soul
When you listen to the air
You will fulfil your heart
And forever you will make it back home
When you listen to the air
You forsake the kink of the dark
And you let yourself open to your codes
It is time to forsake forgetting who you are
Time to drift in the wind on purpose
It is time to take every care for who you are

To love yourself in guided service.
Where there is air there can be light
It's a gentle circus where butterflies take flight
And just when you think the magic is over
The air breathes light on a four leaf clover

Welcome to Air.

AIR BREATHES LIGHT

Darkness.

First there was a darkness
Everywhere you looked
All you saw was nothing
The light was overlooked
In fact, you couldn't see it
The hiding was so strong
The darkness all consuming
The pain so ever long
It felt as though nothing could change
Others, you'd ask, they'd agree
Until you found light company
That made you want to scream
And more than scream
It made you run
You slowly disappeared
Back into the distant dark again
Familiarity forgotten, smeared
You couldn't see the light looking for you
You couldn't see the love was chasing
You only saw the darkness
Interrupted in a moment by light lasers
But you ran
Into the dark again
Believing this is home
For now you can
For now you can
But eventually to light you must roam
– Running away from oxygen doesn't work

Once in the darkness
Everything consumed
No one knows your suffering
All that is left to you
Once alone in darkness
Nobody else can see
At least that's what you tell yourself
It's really all a dream
For suffering is palpable
And darkness seeps out sides
Even if no one is looking
They'd see it if they tried
They can see the way the light fades
When smiles don't reach your eyes
They see the way your heart changed
You used to love so widely
And that's not to say you can't anymore
I just wonder if you're forgetting
Because under the shadow and lonely long nights
That sun in your heart is still setting
And every single day it will rise
Shining brightly before or behind clouds
You are the one who can blow them away
You're also the one who can set them now
So yes, you're in the darkness
The sun in your heart has to hide
For a reason you might not know yet
For a fear that you'd fail if you tried

But I promise
If it matters
That you aren't alone
We all forget the sun sometimes
The one in our chest
The one in the sky
And we all need a friend to remind us
Let me
The narrator
Whisper to you now
The sun still exists
The sun still exists
– You can't run away from the air inside you

AIR BREATHES LIGHT

If there were only darkness
You wouldn't notice it was dark.
– You know when you can't breathe

Maybe,
Where the light lives,
There's an answer to everything that ever was,
To everything going on,
To everything you need.
Maybe,
Where the light lives,
All of you can be seen.
– Where there is air there can be light

Oh but the dark,
So tempting
So comfortable
So familiar
She's an existential kink
The pain we know
Better when self-inflicted
What we don't see can't hurt us right?
Hiding in the dark
What we don't receive can't hurt us right?
Saying no to love
What we don't perceive can't touch us right?
Ignoring all our boundaries
What we don't understand isn't for us right?
Forgetting we are one
– Not breathing doesn't work

One
Two
Three
Four
How many must we lose to the dark before we realise we don't have to?
Millions
Such is evolution
The light will return.
– Air exists whether we breathe it or not

We can pray
As we do when times are hard
And when is that?
When we are consumed by the dark
Why is that?
Well
My dear
You are looking for the light
Hoping for its return
Begging yourself to remember
Opening yourself to the sun inside
When we pray
We are a little less in the shadow
A little more free
A little less alone
A little more at peace
Follow your prayers
– Praying for breath works

ELLIE ANN DEIGHTON

One day they will speak back to you
The prayers you have been speaking
They'll return
A voice in the night
A knowing in the belly
A taste in the mouth
A sound in the air
You'll know.
You'll doubt for a moment:
This is intangible
Could it be so?
Am I really hearing this?
Am I okay?
Perhaps I need more sleep
Is this real?

I'm sure I already knew
This was going to happen
Am I losing it?
Am I losing me?
And then ignore the voice
Return to the dark
Wonder why nothing changes
Tell yourself you're wrong
The air doesn't whisper
Your heart isn't a sun
You aren't a colour
You are only the absence of light
Right?
Little liar, you are sometimes.
– Air doesn't lie

One day the prayer will speak back to you
And you will receive it
And I don't just mean you will
Hear it
Taste it
Smell it
See it
Touch it
Perceive it
I mean you will act on it
You will become one with the prayer returned to you
Your body on the altar table
One with the world
Ready and able to engage in life
And you'll see
The light isn't gone
It was inside you all along
Simply waiting
For the day you choose to listen
– The first deep breath in a while

Today is the day you listen
Today is the day you get your life back
Back from where?
From hiding behind the clouds, my dear.
You've been behind the clouds.
– A second deep breath follows

'You are light, did you forget?'
Well, I guess so.
I guess no one ever told me
No one credible at least
My mum used to whisper in my ear
But she's meant to
So it doesn't count
My dad said, 'Good job'
But I was born to his encouragement
So it doesn't count
My friends say nice things
But they're meant to be nice
So I don't receive it
And strangers can be kind
But that's the world now
We must be polite
Mustn't ruffle feathers
So who knows what's real?
Is anything real other than the breeze on my cheeks?
I can feel that
But I can't touch it between my fingers
'Kind of like the light'
Kind of like the light...
The air I can feel only when I reach out
The light I can feel only when I reach out
– Breathing through fingers

It is dark here
Because I've turned the light off
And there is a voice inside me
Telling me to remember
We aren't saving electricity here
We are living
'Turn the light on'
Okay,
I'll turn the light on.
– My lungs expand and my wings open

Lightness.

I turned the light on
And it hurt so bad
Casting away the darkness
But the darkness has been my skin
My blanket
My safe space
And now I feel naked
Exposed
Terrified
This isn't how it's meant to be
The light is meant to be fun
Living is meant to be liberating
I thought if the light returned so would I
I didn't realise the light shone on the pain
I didn't realise air speaks truth
– My wings retracted

So I turned the light off
Relief flooded over me
And then the grief came
The grief of failure
Of not doing what I said I would
I thought I came here to be myself
Like that was the point of my life
But when the light turned on
I lost control of all I could see in the dark
Which wasn't much
But it was mine
My chaos
My shadow
My unspokenness
And here I am
In the dark again
In the middle of my chaos
Wishing I could reach out
Knowing that the light brings pain
– My wings long to stretch

'Yes, but the pain is proof you are alive, my child'
A voice in my head
It speaks familiarly
As though I've heard the words a million times
Muttered in the same gentle tones
Soothing to my soul
And yet I don't want to believe them
I can feel the truth ringing in my mind's eye
The pain is me alive
I reach out
Flick the switch
Scream
This is what it means to be alive
This is what it means to feel
– Let my wings burn, let me open

The pain consumes me
And then it doesn't
I let it all in
As if impossible
I black out in the light
Losing consciousness for a moment
Overwhelmed by the pain between my eyes
My forehead tingles
Stings
I open my eyes
And I can see a tree with a butterfly on its leaves
Dancing between branches
Pausing
Wings still softly, slowly dancing
Everything else ceases to exist
There's just me and the light between the butterfly wings
I can almost feel the little ripples of wind she's making
This is what I've been missing
– Life is in the light

A car drives past
Butterfly gone
Empty street
A whole world out there with the light on
Dare I wander out into the breeze?
– Light seems delicate

AIR BREATHES LIGHT

To close the door
Or open the window
I will never know
Until I do
And then I know for sure
And I can always change my mind later
To walk
Or to run
Maybe, to dance
There's sunlight in the distance
And it's touching me here too
But it seems there's only one way to go
One foot in front of the other
Wherever my feet find me
I'll give this living in the light thing a go
– Deep breath, single step

ELLIE ANN DEIGHTON

Dark.

ELLIE ANN DEIGHTON

Did you know it's cold out here?
The wind blows into everything.
– Air strips me clear

You can't escape it once you see the truth
It'll haunt you
Until you act on it
And even when you do
You'll never know how it'll change your life
But oh how the truth makes you sing
Unless of course
You ignore it
– Air isn't silence

They don't know your story
But they might be interested if you tell them
It might be none of their business
But you could still keep your heart open
It might be totally out of control
But you can still choose your response
It might be dark
But you can still bring the light
If you want.
– Sing, little bird

Light follows the want
Dark does too
Which want is stronger?
Take a look around you
Can you change your mind?
Dear, of course you can.
Start with,
What's the difference
Between a light or dark human?
Don't make either wrong
We all have our own path
Your job is not to judge yourself
It's to find the path in your heart
If the path is dark now that's okay
It doesn't have to stay
You can let the light fold out of you
It can be safe to play
Even if you feel you're not afraid
If the world is dark, you are
You don't have to cure every one of your fears,
To find the light, just a spark
The darkness can wash over you
And you can still see the light
The darkness can consume you
And you can still find stars in the night.
— Deep breath and stars or shallow sounds and emptiness

What are stars
If not wishes?
Piercing through eternity
Reminding you time isn't real
And you can have it all
Or maybe they're simply gas.
– Delusional or deep breath, not sure

AIR BREATHES LIGHT

Dark isn't bad,
It isn't about shade or colour,
The thing that hurts us in the dark
Is our own denial
Of the light we breathe
Of the light we were born with
Of the light we carry
We all have darkness and that's okay
But it's no good if we ignore that we all have light too
– Light and dark aren't separate and neither are we

Did I mention darkness isn't about colour?
But light refracts the whole rainbow.
Dark is what we get when we close our eyes
Closing our eyes can be awesome!
It's not all bad
It's all a part of us
But it's not all of us
This is what must be remembered
It's okay to journey into the dark
It's okay to want to play there
It's okay to resist the light
It's even okay to forget it
But when the calling comes
When the moment arrives
When the light speaks
You must remember to listen
Must, that is, if fulfilment is important to you in this existence.
– Air breathes light, light breeds fulfilment

Ah, but don't be fooled
Fulfilment comes in the dark too
When we accept our power
When we realise we have a heart
When we realise that which we deny
That which is hiding in the darkness
That which we must journey into the dark to find
We can bring the light with a whole new power.
You see,
I am afraid of people
There it is
I've said it
But when I pretend I'm not afraid of people
It is much more scary
When I let myself
When I see my fears
When I acknowledge what I want to deny
People aren't so scary anymore
Because I fear people in their ability to take the light from me
And I realise
On the other side of my denial
My light *is* me
No one can take it
– Breathing isn't having no more fears

ELLIE ANN DEIGHTON

Light.

Light
Pours out of you
And you know it's true
Because it's happened before
When you were a child and you made up a game
These are the rules!
This is your imagination!
The light was folding out of you
Supporting your imagination
Being your imagination
When you fell in love and didn't know what to do
But you found yourself following your heart anyway
That was your light
When you made a mistake and you told the truth
That was your light
When you forgave them for hurting you
That was your light
When you realised they hurt you because they were hurting themselves
That was your light
When you said yes to looking after yourself, letting yourself rest
That was your light
When you said yes to pushing yourself outside your comfort zone in the pursuit of a dream
That was your light
All of these moments
Maybe they seem incidental
But they're not!

AIR BREATHES LIGHT

That extra one thousand steps you do

That's your light edging you forward

That extra one thousand words you write

That's your light edging you forward

That extra kiss you give

That's you sharing the light

Let it pour

Let it pour

Let it pour

– In with the air, in with the light, up goes the magic

Maybe if you share more of the light
Others will do the same
Maybe the more light you allow to swim out of you
The more light you'll awaken in others
Not because it's your job
It is not your responsibility to turn on others' light
However
It is possible
It is simple
It can be easier and easier to be yourself
Then it's easier and easier to shine in the light
And then the world gets brighter
You are an inspiration, more than you'd ever think
You sharing your light
Tells the world to up the brightness
And there's nothing quite like seeing others turn their light on
To encourage you to be gorgeously happy
– Your light helps me breathe deeper

They say happy people aren't mean
Because they're happy
I'll say happy people have the light on
And they see the world this way
There's no reason to want to see others dim
Because the world is celebrated and bright
There's no reason to want anything but love
And to love when others express all the light
– Happiness dances with deeper breath

They say light unfolds
And I've come to learn it's true
The more I let the light breathe
The more I can share with you
The more I let the air breathe up
The safer I feel on the ground
The more I let the air breathe down
The clearer I feel all around
If light unfolds every time you grow
And growing is all we really do
Then the light coming out is the easiest thing
Easy like me being me, you being you
– Flowers bloom into light but they start in the darkness

Flowers bloom into light but they start in the darkness
Right?
Right
So why must you be perfect all the time
When nature says
You are inherently both?
You are inherently the dark
It is with you,
It can swallow you,
It can become you,
And death is important,
Part of the cycles,
The harvest wouldn't come the following year
If the apple tree didn't shed its leaves
If we didn't offer the tree a trim
If we didn't let the cycle flow through
So why?
Let me tell you:
Because we're judging ourselves.
Why must we be in the light all the time
Or
Be defined as inherently bad?
Judging
Judging
Judging
Scared of what other people think
Scared of what that enemy in the mirror thinks
Scared of losing face

Scared of being misinterpreted
Scared of the light shining so brightly it burns others
Even though we know it burns the hate away
Even though we know it only burns the forgetting
Even though we know our light is the way
We judge ourselves
And we mustn't judge ourselves for judging ourselves
We must simply see
Ah,
We are human
We are pained
We are flawed
We are mistakes in action sometimes
And we are wonderful
We are doing our best
We are taking self-responsibility
And deep, deep breaths
And everything is better on the other side of a few deep breaths
Or a nap
Because what happens when you nap?
You breathe
Unfiltered
You breathe
And then you wake up and you can see clearly again
So remember to be a flower
Be an apple tree
Have your harvest
And come to full bloom

And let yourself wilt
Let autumn come
Let the leaves fall when it is time
Rest
Be still
Nap
Breathe
Lie dormant
Then rise
Into the light
As the light
Breathing deeply
For nature is the way
And this is your nature
– Air is the reason our cells shine and we receive air when we breathe

Nobody is telling you
Or maybe they are
Maybe lucky you!
But maybe nobody is telling you
Pause
Stop
Slow down
Take a deep breath
You don't have to leap right now
Not right now, you're scared
Not right now, you're not breathing
Not right now, you're not really here
Where are your wings?
Breathe into your wings
Let them spread
Let your spine soften
Drop your jaw, stop clenching together
Open your eyes
Deep breath
You can look into me not through me now
You can look into life not through it now
Another deep breath
Wow, there you are
The heart opened
The body softened
The sex opened
The mind softened
You are here

Now you can
Now you know
Now you can
Now you do
– Air helps you to be you

Air helps you to be lighter
You aren't meant to be heavy
Feel the world on your shoulders
You are not Atlas
This is not your punishment
You aren't at fault for being in this life
You are not wrong here
You are simply not breathing
Maybe you aren't breathing for if you do you will cry
For if you do you will see the truth
For if you do you won't want to be here anymore
You will want to break up
You will want to get married
You will have to face the grief
You will feel the raging anger
You will see the path so clearly
You will collide with the truth in your heart
You will no longer deny yourself
And that's the point
– Air breathes truth

Denying yourself never got you anywhere
Except for limitation
Except for shrinking
Except for grief
Except for numbing
Except for shitty relationships
Except for a living mistake
Except for regrets
And sure
Every moment can be an opportunity to redirect
Every breath a chance to get back on your path
– Why don't you start breathing now?

Who are you?
– Stop pretending you don't know

The light is who you are
The light is speaking to you
The dark is here too
Neither is a problem
– You have all the oxygen you need

'You are light, don't you remember?'
– Yes, in the bottom of my lungs, underneath the grief

AIR BREATHES LIGHT

'You are light, didn't you realise that already?'
Mum shakes her head
She can't believe I don't see it
Clare waves her arms
She can't make a big enough tornado
Everybody sees who's looking
They're not all looking
I see the ones who aren't
I lose myself for a minute
Then I see the ones who are
Who see my light
Who see who I really am
Even on the days I don't
And I think to myself
I've got to keep this light around me
Not because I'm not light myself
Because on the days I don't remember
I want the tornado
– Air is in others too

Tornados have a superpower
Generally speaking
Tornados only last for two or three minutes
Can you imagine?
Maybe you've seen one
Two or three minutes
But the whole world changes
Houses are demolished
Homes gone
People killed
Timelines shifts
Realities crushed
Everything changes
What really matters comes to the surface
Love declarations begin
Breakups to follow
The truth rips through just like the air did
Tornados kind of sound like intuition
Like an awakening
Has it happened to you?
You know the feeling
All these baby signs
Synchronicities
They've been happening
Building
Maybe you don't even notice the change in the weather
Or you do,
But you don't think much of it

And then
The tornado strikes
All the pieces come together
You realise they were all warnings
Clues of the clarity to come
It isn't necessarily bad
But the ego doesn't like change
The world changes
The old you dies
In the moment you see the truth
The past is dead to you
It has to be
And then there's grief
But it doesn't touch the liberation of the truth
The house didn't fit you anymore anyway
They weren't your person
You were kidding yourself
Playing small
Forgetting the light
And just like that
The roof is blown off
The sunlight floods in
You drown in it
But underneath the wreckage
Right there bathing in the sun
Suddenly you breathe
– An awakening of air

Waking up
Is like taking the glasses off
And realising you can still see
In fact you can see better
You could see all along
And now you may feel a little stupid
But you'll get over it
Because what you can see is liberation
– Air breathes clarity

Shimmering.

They say focus creates your reality
Focus creates my reality
That's a terrifying thing
Because I've created terrifying things
Now I know all my worst thoughts will become real
Now I am all upside down and sideways,
Worried about my thoughts and feelings,
Which creates a lot more thoughts and feelings,
Which is a worry.
– I can *just* see my light but I don't believe in it

If I worry enough,
Maybe I can control the thoughts and feelings,
Maybe I can stop
The beasts from turning into my reality
Maybe I can resist
Dwelling in this worry
Ha
No
I cannot
– Focusing on the absence of light constricts my breath

If focus creates my reality,
Maybe I can use it to my advantage
Maybe I can focus on where the light has been
Maybe I can remember who I am
When the light is on
Inside of me
There is a light
Inside of me
There it is!
– Focus on the light, you'll see the light

Now I see the light
It's inside of me
A little shimmer
I'm not sure what it's doing
Flickering like a flame
Blowing about like a little eddy
Wriggling around
Like it's unsure of its existence
– The light isn't unsure, you are

Now it's flickering so much
This little light in me
I wonder
Will it flicker out?
– It doesn't flicker out, you look away from it

AIR BREATHES LIGHT

I've looked away
From the light
Into the abyss
It's a never ending darkness
Without that light
When the lights are off
Creatures come to play
But they aren't the creatures of my dreams
They are the creatures of nightmares
They are the creatures that freeze me in this spot
They are the creatures that touch me and I rot
They are the creatures that make me feel alone
They are the creatures that stop me coming home
To my heart
The place of the light
Although I try
With all my might
The creatures are there
And I can't look away
Their eyes have me trapped
I don't know what to say
There's nothing to say, it appears
Nothing true
They're simply here with me
Stopping me from following through
They know there's a calling
In my heart
To write

To sing and to dance
To cherish and to be
Whoever I want
Whoever I need
Hey, there's the light!
It has come back!
I just had to pull some weeds
For the light's always there
That's what I am learning
And the creatures block them when I ask them to
My dark focus filled with yearning
To prove that I'm not good enough
That I'm filled with disbelief
That's what I find in all the dark
It fills me up with grief
And when the grief lands
It tells me what to do
Stop writing!
She screams
I comply, it feels like truth
Stop living!
She yells,
And that's that
That's what I'll do
And so I've learnt
I have to let go
Of the deep need to listen
To the grief that comes and goes

AIR BREATHES LIGHT

I have to lean into
Expecting the light
And sometimes it feels like
One heck of a fight
But when I lean in
The light is always there
Like a gentle, soft whisper
And a tickle in my hair
The whisper will come
And the light I will see
And I know it's light talking,
Because it tells me to be me
– The light is always there - look for it

ELLIE ANN DEIGHTON

Glimmering.

A glimmer

Is a moment of hope

A moment designed to make you smile

To take the worry off your shoulders

So you can rest a while

To remind you this life

Isn't supposed to be so hard,

A reminder this life

Is often filled with charm

A glimmer is a moment

That reminds you what life is about

It can jolt you out of your pity party

It can make you scream and shout

I am alive!

Yes,

I'm glad that you remember

That glimmer

Will sing to you

October to September

All year round

As the wheel turns

You'll have countless invitations

To let the light burn

And it doesn't burn you painfully

It burns you back home

Like a light that is weaved by a torchbearer

A light that lives in hope

That you will cast your focus on it

AIR BREATHES LIGHT

And listen to what it says
For your next step is always sitting there
In the light and its gentle haze
When you see the light, you can feel it
Let it wash now over you
Like a breeze that's bringing freshness
Suddenly you know what to do
And in the light that's guiding you
You will find your kingdom comes
Or yes, it can be a queendom
The point is that it comes
And when you forget the light
You can come back to see
That air is still now flowing
Blowing kisses back to thee
Thee is you, by the way, it's old talk
And it's telling us nothing new
This wisdom inside you is ancient and weird
Filled with rainbow gifts for you
The light, if you let it, is like the yellow brick road
If you stray, you can get back on
Keep an eye out for glimmers
For moments that show
You the way
And you'll never be lost
– The glimmers are always on the breeze - listen to them, look for them, receive them.

Sometimes you'll hold your breath for too long
You'll forget the glimmer
You'll be pulled into darkness
Suffocated in the heaviness of winter
But sometimes, you see,
Winter isn't bad!
It's nourishment and rest and gentle
The best reminder you've ever had
See when you fall
Into the darkness
It doesn't mean you've failed.
It means you need a reminder to breathe
And perhaps
You're distracted because it's hailed
It's cold
The conditions aren't right
Or so they seem
But breathing is still available.
And rather,
The more you breathe,
Just getting started,
Can be enough to let you out of gaol
For the gaol isn't real
It's completely of your mind
Even though evidence is everywhere you look
That focus is creating your reality again
Think it's best that you read a different book?
Yes,

AIR BREATHES LIGHT

I do,
Let's look for the light,
For all the reasons you *can* breathe
Because you love it
Because you want to
Because the sky calls to you
If only you are willing to receive it
So,
Little breather,
When life feels stormy
Know that the sea breeze can change
It's not all gloom
You're certainly not doomed
Just your focus is clouded in a haze
You don't need to find perfection
To find your way out
All you need is a glimmer of light
You can feel the air pick you up
Whisper you home
You can breathe
And it can be a delight
– The breeze is always speaking to you - listen again.

'Do they help you shine more brightly?'
The tools you use
The teachers you choose
The friends you seek
The lovers you keep
They either turn you on
Or turn you off
Triggers can be golden
But triggers are different to squashing
Light squashers can change their ways
But it's not your job to change them
– Live where you can breathe deeply

A glimmer

Is a faint sign or feeling

A desirable one

That reminds you that you're alive

And there is good here

A faint or wavering light,

A pretty one

That reminds you that there's beauty

And there is magic here

– You notice glimmers when you breathe

ELLIE ANN DEIGHTON

Shine.

ELLIE ANN DEIGHTON

Where you can breathe deeply
You can shine
The rest can be learnt as you go
Air breathes light
– You are the light

'Do they help you see the light?'
When your eyes glaze over
And the clouds overcome you
And you are immersed in the memory of pain
And you can't seem to find a way out
And you reach out your hand
And you're asking for help
And you don't have it in you to use words
But your body is a full expression of where you are at
Do they see?
Do they take your hand?
Do they show you back to the light?
This friend
This lover
This teacher
These folk
Do they remind you of the power you are?
Because you are
This light inside you is a super power
Sometimes you will forget it
That's part of being human
But your people
Your real, true people
Will help you remember
– Your soul people will show you the light in you

We aren't meant to shine alone
And we certainly aren't shining for the sake of hurting people
We will shine so brightly
When we accept our light
That it will have the crusts of darkness crumble off the others
And they might not like it
For it isn't comfortable
Being exposed
Feeling naked in the light for the first time in a while
Maybe in a long time
But afterwards
One day
Many years later
It could be
There will come a time
They are thankful that you shone the light
And even if not
I dare you to shine anyway
Because your shining serves others in quitting their shrinking
And your shrinking does nothing but shrink
– Shine baby, shine

There is no way
You were born
To be this beautiful
And this bright
And turn the light off
– Your light is meant for shining

ELLIE ANN DEIGHTON

It isn't possible
To cut you off from breath
And stop you being who you are
– The soul light lives forever

AIR BREATHES LIGHT

Air is when
You're in the supermarket
And there are so many options
And you take a breath
And the options for you light up
– Light goes in the basket

Air is when
You're on the treadmill
Heart racing
Legs burning
Lungs begging
And you look up to your muse to ask:
Do I go on?
And your muse slices through all your fears of hurting
The fear of pushing too much
And slices through your tendency to overdo it
To use up all the oxygen at your own expense
And you follow your guidance
You move in alignment with your guidance
Because you've cultivated a relationship with it
And you know

Without a shadow of a doubt
This movement muse speaking to you
Really it's just your soul
When your soul says, *yes*
You go
Push on
Break all your self-imposed limits
And when your soul says, *rest*
You stop
Pause
Let yourself be
Celebrate your progress
Nourish yourself
Because you can have it all
– Light only damages the ego

It's a funny thing
When we realise we are shining
And we let ourselves
– Suddenly we can breathe again

It's a dangerous thing
When we realise we are shining
And we dim the lights
– Suddenly we aren't being ourselves

Funny how reflections show us the light dancing
If we look ahead, we can see which path has the light
If we look back, we can see if the way we went was the way of light
If we look down, we can see if our feet are planted in light
And if we are willing to notice
The question becomes
Are we willing to create change?
Are we willing to double down on the light and shine?
Are we willing to step out of the shadow and into the golden bath and shine?
Are we willing to follow our light even when others don't approve?
Can we follow the light even when we have doubt?
Can we take the step even if it's illogical?
Can we say yes to our soul when our mind screams no?
Can we let love in even after we have been hurt?
Can we let the light touch the edges it's never touched before?
Can we expand into a new level of abundance where we shine more brightly?
Can we be seen in the light?
Will I let you see me in the light?
Will I let you see me?
Can I see you?
– Air says yes

AIR BREATHES LIGHT

I would love
To look into your eyes
And see the light flicker there
Hold onto the moment
Smile at you
See the light expand through your face
When you smile back
The energy is like a hug
A warmth spreads through
It's like when the sun peeks through the clouds
Everything is clear again
The air fresher
The wind a new delight
The light spread between and of us
– Love is all around and so is air

ELLIE ANN DEIGHTON

Everywhere we look
And everywhere we don't look
Air is always available
– It's up to us to choose to breath

AIR BREATHES LIGHT

Everywhere we look
And everywhere we don't look
Light is always shining
– It's up to us to open our eyes (all three of them)

ELLIE ANN DEIGHTON

Butterflies come from the goop
From the darkness of the cocoon
But they fly out into the light
They spread their wings in flight
– If caterpillars evolve and butterflies shine so can you

AIR BREATHES LIGHT

Even creatures who see in the dark
Do so because they are more sensitive to light
– There is always light shining if you're attuned to it

Air breathes light
Because when we follow our guidance
We become who we truly are
And really
Underneath it all
Beyond the flesh
We are light
– And our intuition knows it

AIR BREATHES LIGHT

It's important to note
That just because the air can be a gentle breeze
Doesn't mean it can't be a wild tornado
Sometimes the air gives us the medicine we need,
The message we've been avoiding,
The cliff we've delayed jumping off
Because we are afraid we won't grow wings
But we have wings
And they grow when we engage them
And when we are served a tornado dose of intuition
Everything that isn't serving us blows away
Everything we clung to with our ego melts
And we are given the opportunity to walk a clearer path
To start a new story
To embrace the level of our hearts
And this new story?
Sometimes it's not a story we think we want
Often it's certainly *not* comfortable
To live one with the air means to change form
To change form means to let go of the known
But wow
When we follow the thread of light left in the wake of the storm
We find our dreams come true
– Air carries truth and fulfilment comes when we are one with it

So our greatest pursuit becomes
To shine our light
Over and over
Even when others try to dim it
Even when our wounds try to dim it
Even when we're told we're too much
Even when... anything
Air tells us
Clearly, softly and fiercely
Unconditionally
Intuition knows the way
– Our purpose is to shine in the direction of our guidance (I call this shining guided)

If we shine guided
We can do no wrong
Not because we can't make mistakes
Not because we won't ever get nervous
But because our guidance never leads us astray
Sure, sometimes it leads us to learning
But learning to be ourselves in a world that says no to our shining...
That's a beautiful, light, very important thing
– Breathe deeply, shine brightly

They say air is like the soft masculine
Whispering to you gently
Holding you
Encouraging you
Having faith in your ability to choose your gifts
Confident that you will recognise your strengths
Humble enough to know not everything has to be for us
Loving without judgement
But what if the air is just you
Whispering you home
Showing you the way
Guiding you back to your light
Letting you know everything is going to be okay
Wondering where you've been and so glad you're back
Hoping you see how magical you are
Patient enough to wait until you do see
Persistent enough to hold until you do see
What if the air is the light unfolded out of you
Bouncing back
Edging you forward at the exact perfect pace for you and your heart
Encouraging you in just the way you need
And maybe, yes, like the perfect father
But maybe, also, like the perfect mother
And also, mostly, like the perfect inner voice?
– Air is you

Whole.

If you could remember
The air is you
An expression of your guidance
The language of your heart
An unfolding of light
The perfect place to start,
If you could remember
Like the sky is blue
The air is a mirror
Here to take you home
To tell you of your beauty
And help you conquer your own
Trolls that might distract you now
From the path of light you tread
You might just now remember

AIR BREATHES LIGHT

You were born to love instead
Of paying bills
And existing
And paying more bills
And surviving
And buying obligatory gifts
And begging
To be a good person
And trying
You might remember
If you were willing to listen
That the air is you
Telling you how to be the person you were born to be
– Air assumes you have it in you to be you

If you have it in you
To be yourself
And you also have it in you
To forget yourself
Wouldn't it be great
To always have a reminder
Of which you'd rather choose?
– Air reminds you if you let it

AIR BREATHES LIGHT

When you walk outside
And the breeze kisses your face
– Air is reminding you to be you

ELLIE ANN DEIGHTON

When you're in your bed
And your loved one breathes on you
– Air is reminding you to receive love

When you're in the ocean
And you step out into the cold
– Air is reminding you you're alive

ELLIE ANN DEIGHTON

When you can't see through the fog
But you slowly know the way
– Air is reminding you it isn't always logical

When you hear the storm outside
And the creaks of giant trees
– Air is reminding you of your inner strength

When you blow out the candle
And the ritual is complete
– Air is reminding you that you direct it

AIR BREATHES LIGHT

When you turn the fan on
And the smoke clears
– Air is reminding you that the answer is always available

ELLIE ANN DEIGHTON

When you take a deep breath
And push it through an echo chamber
– Air is reminding you that your soul has a song

AIR BREATHES LIGHT

When you realise your breath is stuck in your chest
And you let it down into your belly
– Air is reminding you to be grounded here on Earth

ELLIE ANN DEIGHTON

When you are filled with doubt
But you clearly see the way before you
And you leap
– Air is reminding you that magic will catch you

AIR BREATHES LIGHT

When you're not sure
And you ask your heart
– Air is the language of intuition

ELLIE ANN DEIGHTON

When you feel your feelings
And then the storm clears
– Air can get through to you now

When you've had an argument
And realised you don't have to be right
– Air reminds you to choose love over righteousness

When you've had a prayer come true
And you realise you did it
– Air reminds you that your dreams are soul whispers

When you go to the place
Where only your soul speaks
And you've told everyone else:
The internalised voice of your mum
Or your teacher
Of your grandfather
Or a preacher,
You don't belong here...
You can be here with me
But you can't drive me
You can be a part of my story
But you can't end my story
You can be an opinion
But you don't get the final vote
You can be the majority
But I am the biggest investor in my world
You can think differently
But that doesn't make me wrong
You can be disgusted
But that doesn't make you right
You can be shocked
But that doesn't make this a mistake
You can be delighted
But that doesn't mean I'm doing it for you
Because you're in the soul place now
The soul has the steering wheel
Your soul has the steering wheel
And everyone else can be on the train

But you laid the tracks
And you can change direction
And you decide when to stop
And you can press go again
And there's no such thing as a soul dream you can't have
There's only:
Are you willing to listen to your soul
Over all the other noise?
Are you willing to lead your life from your wholeness
And accept that you'll be human while you're at it?
– Air doesn't need you to fix yourself

AIR BREATHES LIGHT

If you filled your lungs with light
Would you be surprised if breathing felt easier?
— It isn't meant to be hard to be yourself (but it will be if you fight it)

ELLIE ANN DEIGHTON

If every time you were honest
Light poured in
And every time you lied to yourself
The light dimmed
How bright would you be?
– You hold the light dial

I wrote once in a workbook in 2021:

Air,

The intellect
Requires an acknowledgement
Before a feeling
Requires a listening
Before a healing
Requires a moment,
A breath,
A forgiveness of the noise.
The whispers in the trees
Bring me to my knees
The whispers on my face
Bring me into ease
Light fills the darkness
If only I can be willing to listen
Breath fills my body
If only I let it in
Air
The window to my intuition
Keeper of my keys
Giver of my clarity
Holder of my heart
She wants him to hold
To anchor,

ELLIE ANN DEIGHTON

> To acknowledge,
> To celebrate,
> To be,
> With all that air is singing,
> And mostly,
> The reminder to be me.

And quite frankly,

I was onto something.

– Air blows out the shit and reminds you to just be yourself

If all else fails
Remind yourself that you are whole
And keep going
– Air won't let you quit (even if you already have)

Even if you've already quit
You can start again
It doesn't have to be over
You don't have to give up on your dreams
You can decide that wasn't the last step
It was just a side step
A pausing step
A learning step
And then you can learn and move on
And if you keep going
Maybe all your dreams will come true
And you'll realise you were whole the whole time
Even when you believed you were broken
Because there was air in your lungs
And you were doing your best
And you learnt from it
And sometimes learning and moving forward is all we can do
And sometimes we wallow for a while before we remember
– Not an excuse, just a reminder that air can be gentle too

AIR BREATHES LIGHT

We don't want to pat ourselves on the back
For every time we've been a pansy
And wussed out of what was calling us
Dulled down the truth
Snuffed out the candle prematurely
Told ourselves we couldn't
But we do want to remember
We don't always get it right the first time
Sometimes the 'failures' are simply the best learnings
Often that thing you learnt from that time you failed lifts you onto the next level
You have to run at any speed before you can sprint
When you were a baby you learnt to crawl
And now look at you!
– One breath at a time makes up a whole life

My wish for you
Is to remember you are guided
At any moment
There is a light
You can see it
You do know
You will remember
You feel one with it
You are your true self
– Air breathes light

Air breathes light
What does that mean?
It means it'll flush you out
Wake you up
Energise you
Remind you: you are whole!
Energise you
Connect you to your people
Energise you
Align you to your purpose
Unfold out of you
Open you
Remind you: this is the way!
Tease you until you claim the way
Pick you up when you've been feeling down
Did I mention: flush you out
Empty out the crap
Free you of heavy feelings
Expand what you knew was possible
Wake you up
Transform you into yourself
You get it
Your intuition won't lead you astray
– Air breathes light

Once you learn your intuitive language
It's like the piano of instruments
Now the world is your oyster
Now any vision is possible
Now you can transfer your skills to wherever you like
Trombone?
Have a go!
Violin?
Okay, here it is!
Harmonica?
Why not?
You can play any instrument now
But you don't have to play every instrument
You play the ones you are called to
Life after learning piano looks like
Choosing the playlist for the rest of your life
And everybody loves music
– Air is universal but you still have your own tone

I have a friend
Who finds herself
When she rolls over
Folds over
Into the foetal position
Suddenly
All the information
Every answer
Each piece she needed
It's right there
– She found her air, so can you

Maybe you naturally feel it
Maybe you see it
Maybe you hear it
Maybe you just 'get' it
Maybe you can't explain it, but here's your decision
Maybe one felt warm and the rest cold and that's how you knew,
It doesn't matter how
It matters that you recognise it
– Learn to see the air for what it is and follow your guidance

AIR BREATHES LIGHT

Guidance is useless
If all you do is ignore it
− You need to breathe, my friend

ELLIE ANN DEIGHTON

It doesn't matter
If you never tell anyone
It matters
If you follow the language of your heart
– You don't have to translate your air, you have to live it

AIR BREATHES LIGHT

If I imagine myself as whole
Really whole
Really full of light
Really doing my best
Really living in and from my heart
Really grounded in my chest
Everything falls into place
It isn't hard to be open
I can love anyone
Even if I don't agree
I can accept anything
Even if it doesn't promote peace
Because I know I'm on my path
Because I know I'm playing my part
Because I know my soul's expression
Is my greatest gift and my greatest lesson
Because I know if I commit to my heart's shine
The pain will soon dissolve
Because I know one heart at a time
I can lift other people up
And that's the point really
Air breathes light
And air breathes up
Lifts us up
Helps us fly
Raises the vibration
Shows us a lighter way
Shows us something different

ELLIE ANN DEIGHTON

Allows the possibilities to float in
Reminds us we don't have to figure out everything
We just have to remember who we are
We just have to remember who we are
I just have to remember who I am
– Air equals light equals love

If I just be me
And you just be you
And we just encourage others to do the same
Everyone will be taken care of
– We all belong in a light-filled world
– Everyone has a heart
– We all have oxygenated blood
– We are all connected through all of space and time

Enlightenment says
When we ascend we aren't here anymore
Until then
Let's do our best
– Humans need to breathe

Everybody says
They just knew that was going to happen!
I knew it was going to be you!
I had a feeling you'd be here!
I thought this would happen soon!
I've been thinking of you and here you are!
This is perfect timing, what a coincidence!
Wow, what a synchronicity!
So isn't it possible that we're all magic?
– There is magic in the air

There is magic in the air
And if you let it
It will fill your cells
And before you know it
You'll be flying
No broomstick necessary
It'll be you in the clouds with the sun and the stars
It'll be up to you which direction you travel
And who you visit
And where you spend your time
And how much it costs you to get there
And you'll get faster at flying
And you'll work out that you're invisible to some
And an inspiration to many
And you'll show them they can fly too
In your own special way
Because there will be a way you can explain it
A way you can share this magic
And before you know it
You'll be surrounded by people you love in the air
Strangers turn into best friends
Because they see you
And they just get it
And other people will get heavier and heavier
They'll nail their feet to the ground
Scream at you that the devil has overcome you
And you'll shed a tear for them in compassion

And laugh for them because you've been subject to the cosmic joke too
And you'll fly more
Until you'll see there are people flying around with healing feet
They saw through the illusion of their heaviness
They released themselves from their self-imposed shackles
For there is magic in the air
And maybe it wasn't you who reminded them to breathe
It was a friend of a friend of a stranger of a friend of a stranger
And it doesn't matter
It simply matters that there's magic in the air
And more of us are breathing it
And when you forget
And you start to sink
Floating down until your feet hit the earth
A special someone will whisk past and plant you with a kiss
And you'll remember
There's magic in the air
We aren't meant to do it alone
We can help each other remember
Everything is going to be better than okay
You are loved
On the earth and in the sky
– Air is whispers of love whenever we need them

ELLIE ANN DEIGHTON

The Wheel Of Life
The Epilogue

Air comes first
Sweeps us off our feet
Reminds us who we are
Helps us speak our own language
Untangles us from the remnants of somebody else's patterning
Shows us the essence of it
Of life
Of us
Of the language of our heart
And all the ways we can interpret it
And all the ways it promotes connection
And suddenly everything is easier
– Air breathes light

Second comes the flame
That reminds us we are alive in a body
One with our flesh
Here for loving and love making
Here to burn through and overcome our shame
Here to plant embers for forever in our hearth
Here to receive
Here to conceive
Here to be
– Fire breathes life

Third comes the water
Reminding us to move
To let the rivers run their course
To find the ocean
To sink into the deep
To be one with the seabed and the stars
To allow the waterfalls and the tiny creek beds
To be the pillow of a lake or the flow of a river
To feel
To feel
To feel
– Water breathes alchemy

Then comes the silver
The thread through the stone
The circles we have always stood in
The ashes we have risen from
The sisters we stood next to
The brothers we stood next to
The ones we remember
The remembering
The remembering
The remembering
Of the magic of who we are
And the ancient rituals that brought us here
And the nature that reflects through our very cells
And the Earth that turns
As do our insides
As do our hearts
As do the leaves on the trees
As do our sisters
As do our lovers
As do our lives
– Silver breathes circles

Then comes the gold
The very gifts
And magical talents
That bring us into abundance
When we let them shine
– Gold breathes greatness

Then the salt
Sprinkles through the top of everything
It's the base layer that
Doesn't change
No matter what
No matter who speaks
No matter where life leads
The spirit doesn't dislodge
The spirit doesn't leave
Not really
The salt stays in the cauldron
And our bodies move in response to our spirit
Learning
Seeing
Knowing
Clairvoyant again
– Salt breathes spirit

Finally we come to Earth
Our voices the patterns of the stars
Our missions the eagerness in our bones
Our community right there cheerleading us
Our songs passed through all of time and space
And our last message to the Earth
Captured
Timeless
Stars infinitely grounded
Defying possibility
Embracing oneness
Giving truth
Storytelling
The way of every time and every people
– Earth breathes song

And so it is
The wheel of life
We are all of it
Some of it we do so well
Know so well
Remember so deeply
Some of it we need such help
Lean on others
Forget completely
All of it is in us
– The wheel of life breathes fulfilment

ELLIE ANN DEIGHTON

silver witch rose
out may 2025

A ring of SILVER

First the silver drips
Breaking the illusion
That it is only for royal spoons
And you realise
Quickly
As you look around the circle
And you peer into the stones
You have done this a thousand times
And you'll do it a thousand more
In the name of remembering
– In circle we remember

Silver is calling. Will you respond?
Read ***Silver Witch Rose*** Now

About the author

She teaches humans how to live in the light of their true selves and she goes first.
Like an integrity radar
Through life
Hers and yours
She will find the cracks
And spit them out
Until your world tastes like honey together
For she is not here to walk alone
And neither are you.
It is no mistake that you are here reading this.
Is it stories in her books calling you in for a journey?
Is her music singing you home to the temple of you?
Is her curriculum asking you to become more of yourself?
Is now the time?
I believe so.
The scientist in her has a hypothesis,
That you are magic,
The facilitator in her
Can prove it,

The witch in her
Can give you the tools to cast it,
The woman in her
Can celebrate you as you shine,
The artist in her
Is on stage creating beside you.
You are magic,
And here,
You will find that you are home.
– about Ellie, author of *Air Breathes Light*

Author's note

You will never be alone
For you will always have your air
And light will always be inside you
Beckoning your return to your guided path
You can close your eyes and take a breath
And you can open your eyes and look for the light
And you can place your hands on your body and feel the wisdom
And you can move your body and hear the air whisper
And even on the darkest days
There can be a light
Because of your willingness to be with your air
And the greatest gift you could ever give yourself
Is to learn to
See
Listen
Feel
Receive
Remember
Play
Speak

Be
Air
And let the light shine free
– Air is what I teach

And I can teach you to receive your air too
Or you can receive little air whispers to your inbox

Subscribe for bonuses at <u>elliedeighton.com/air</u>

Intuitively Me
The Wheel Of Life

There is a way
A guided one
That works every time
It works without fail
Because you are connected
To all of time and space
And light cascades through everything
And you can navigate the light with grace
There is a sacred wheel
Of fulfilment and elemental things
And when you embrace your light
It's easy to feel the joy it brings
And actually it's more like peace
It's completely and utterly relaxing
To be one with whom you were born as
And to take off all the masks that are taxing
And to finally be with yourself
To know the difference between thoughts and intuition
And to finally be done with self-help

And lean in for the answers are within
– *Intuitively Me* is the self-paced gift of air

Join Ellie and Clare in *Intuitively Me: The Wheel of Life*, an online self-paced journey into the realm of air and intuitive channeling.

Use the discount code AIRBREATHESLIGHT to begin your journey today.
elliedeighton.com/intuitively-me-air

Acknowledgements

Clare
Mem
William
Mum
Dad
Leah
Jo
Rose
Elissa
Kel
Alex
Paige
Chris
Kalyah
Timothy

– Thank you for sharing your air with me, ***Air Breathes Light*** has been a relaxing undertaking whilst taking deep breaths with you.

www.ingramcontent.com/pod-product-compliance
Lightning Source LLC
Chambersburg PA
CBHW071242070526
44583CB00017B/2293